FALLEN ANGELS

FALLEN ANGELS

Terry Hauptman

Published by North Star Press of St. Cloud
www.northstarpress.com

First Edition

Printed in the United States of America.

ISBN: 978-1-68201-139-3

Praise:

v

"Fallen Angels" is a great example of Terry Hauptman's vision. Fallen-down, Angels-up, and when fallen angels are involved it's through a kind of creative resurrection where the poems carry us through the ethos of hope and the beauty of transformation. Terry's penumbra is about light and shadow equally and the nuanced transitions that unveil radiant and soulful revelations when moving between the two.

'Stepping into the forest's music, the twilight of mystery, the dark light illuminated by pines.' from "Cherish."

There's music in these poems and the harmonies are both major and minor at once. They dwell in our frailties that are entwined with powers of redemption. They are potent expressions of soul that glow to reveal our beauty, spirit, and mortality's greater good."

-Brian Fitzpatrick

"In Terry Hauptman's latest book of poems, *Fallen Angels*, she once again draws from so many sources, inspired by her vast knowledge of world poetry. There are poems about the pandemic, about her daughter, about love, hope, prayer, and dreams, and a number inspired by her friends. Several quote Pablo Neruda's moving verse. Her beautiful use of sounds and imagery, her love for language and art, and her reflections on our contemporary heartache, draws us in. There is a musical quality to Terry Hauptman's poems, one that is both soothing and marvelous. *Fallen Angels* is delightfully eclectic in its inspirations and, as always, a superb collection by a master poet. What a gem of a book!"

-Gerald McBride

"In Terry Hauptman's book, *Fallen Angels*, words sensuous and evocative wash over one like music. These poems are not meant to be dissected, analyzed, but understood at another level. The verses seep into you as incantation, intoxicating, casting a spell that takes you out of the every day and into the numinous Many of the poems are a deep bow of gratitude and love to poets and painters of the past (some well known such as Max Jacob, Pablo Neruda, others less so ,such as Lebanese poet Mahmoud Darwish). Her pantheon is multi-ethnic and broad, and evinces a deeply felt connection to a history of poetry that adds a rich historical background to this collection."

-Arlene Distler.

"We waited with baited breath for *Fallen Angels*, the new book by Terry Hauptman written during the heart of the pandemic. In the midst of death and isolation, her surrealist poems are the voice of angels. They are meant to be sung 'as terror floats and winds break open.' Exquisite lines like 'Blue clay of consciousness' and 'My mother's green humming from her grave today' remind her readers of the psalms of David."

-Toni Ortner

"Terry's voice is that of a Bardic poet; the present and the past resonate in her work. Her natural lyricism is always present and it informs the anger she feels because of all the injustice and loss present in our world. Her feelings are presented in rich, poetic language--a classic is being written, the ongoing disasters from the Covid epidemic are seen in this mode:

> 'Lilacs in the burnt wind
> Spark the soul's migration,
> As we raise the dead communally,
> From the dusk's locked up night.
> We are not alone--nature shares our grief.'

Terry shares her poetry with poetry. Every poem has reference to another poet who stirs her feelings and accompanies her vision--they are visionaries in their craft and in her work. They all "shelter in place" as she makes her predictions:

> 'Dreams will not protect us
> From the poison seeping within.
> Black birds rattle coffins
> In the lies of the day,
> Crows bury the dead
> As all is taken away.'"

-Barbara Clark

"No one else could have written about the pandemic, it's sorrows, as well as what we need to transcend the carnage left in its wake. You have brought the impact of the Pandemic to a spiritual realm you always inhabit with the deepest clarity of feeling, Love and Hope in each poem. The mountain poems, made us feel so lucky to have been there in time and spirit."

-From a letter to Terry by
Hugh and Jeanne Joudry

Dusk falls Raziel, Dusk falls

DEDICATION

Gratitude for the earth womb of winter bees
   Sparking the raven world's hive
Gratitude for the night winds green eyes
   The heart womb of mystery
      As agates split open.

For Kira

If our flaws spark our gifts
From the darkest wounds
Will the blessings of life
Soothe our sorrows?

Into each soul
We enter
To find the
strength
In ourselves

-Jack Herman,
My father

OTHER POETRY BOOKS BY TERRY HAUPTMAN

Masquerading in Clover: Fantasy of The Leafy Fool
Boston: Four Zoas, 1980
(With hand-painted plates).

Rattle
Tulsa: Cardinal Press, 1982
(With an introduction by Meridel LeSeuer)

On Hearing Thunder
St. Cloud, Minnesota: North Star Press, 2004.
(With color plates)

The Indwelling of Dissonance
St. Cloud, Minnesota: North Star Press, 2016

The Tremulous Seasons
St Cloud, Minnesota, North Star Press, 2019

Rubies In The Mud
Polaris Publications, An Imprint of North Star Press, 2021

ACKNOWLEDGEMENTS

"Return," *Poems In The Time of Covid*, Small Pond Press, Brattleboro, Vermont. 2021 *Poems Around Town*, 25. Displayed in Everyone's Books, Brattleboro, Vermont. Bookstore Window for Poets Around Town Project, April, 2021, Recorded on Zoom.

"Pandemic: The Fire In The God's Eyes," *Caliban Online*, Contributor's Advise, 2020, published in *Rubies In The Mud*, North Star Press, MN, 86.

"Wild Sister" First published in *Rattle*, Cardinal Press, Tulsa, OK 1982. Edited by Mary McAnally, with an introduction by Meridel LeSeuer. Blurbs by Joy Harjo and Mary McAnally.

Zooms In The Time of Covid Brattleboro Literary Festival: Write Action Spotlight Reading with Tim Mayo, Toni Ortner, and others, October, 2020.

Brattleboro Literary Festival: Write Action Spotlight Reading, October, 2021.

Manchester Community Library Poetry Salon Zoom with poet Claire North hosting readers: Alice Gilborn, Kiev Rattee, Terry Hauptman, for Poetry Month Event, April, 2021.

Putney Public Library Winter Zoom with Toni Ortner hosting. Poetry with Steve Minkin, Terry Hauptman, January 2022.

"Transcendence," Write Action Newsletter, Spring 2022.

"Daughter of My Soul," Write Action: *Poems Around Town*, April, 2022.

Contents

Heart-Womb 51

DAUGHTER OF MY SOUL

Poem for Kira's Twentieth Birthday

Daughter of my Soul,

   You deepen me,

      With your night roots

      Planted in the azure earth

Tree of Life

   Sacred In The moonlight

   I move towards you

Daughter of my soul

   You deepen me

      Singing love's thunder

         On the dirt road to our home

         Through the dreamtime

Green bird of vision and light

   You deepen me

      Whirl me through serenity's dawn

         As we rise up

         Together in song.

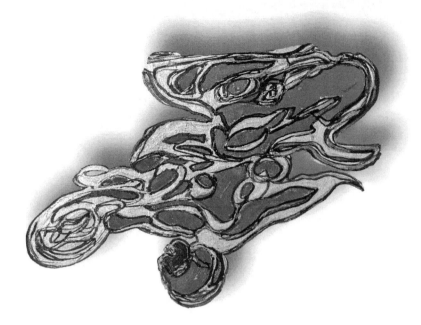

FALLEN ANGELS

Children eat dirt candy
As the new moon
Shelters in place

"Return to the root of the root
of your soul"
-Rumi

FALLEN ANGELS Mixed-Media Painted Scrolls.

As The Pandemic persisted, it was the angels asking questions from the soul that sparked a powerful series of Fallen Angel Mixed-Media Scrolls, one of which appears on the front cover, enhanced by Liz Dwyer's book design, as well as the section breaks. Deepening in inspiration and transformation, as well as grief, I contemplated what was happening, sending a prayer to those who died, or were changed, forever. I found myself connecting to previous tragedies, honoring those who, in crisis, cried out from the abyss of hope.

PANDEMIC: THE FIRE IN THE GODS' EYES

Dead bees rest inside God's fire

As we cherish the night,

Keeping hope alive,

Cherish the night's green winds

Between the shadows'

Exiled song,

The world's grief,

A pandemic of fear.

Light a candle for ancestral prayers,

The lost dreams and mysteries

Never to be shared

Singing deep songs

For the dead and the living

As terror flails

And the winds break open.

SHELTER IN PLACE 1

For Arlene Distler

Here we are
  At the precipice
    As death
      Spirals around us.
        We breathe in the pines,
        The coltsfoot,
            The mountain ash.

Surrender to the dream vision
  Of night and day
    In sorrow we are changed
      As wet-market bats
      Mark our destiny
        Spinning as we
            Shelter in place.

Your night soul
  Inspires my becoming,
  Is music to my silence,
    Telling fortunes,
        If we could speak.

SHELTER IN PLACE 2

For Toni Ortner

"In the dark times

will there be singing?

Yes, there will be singing

About the dark times."

-Bertold Brecht

Fear lives in our spirit house
That lives inside us,
Turns us inward
Towards ourselves
To greet the day.

Children eat dirt candy
As the new moon
Shelters in place.

What will become of us
Singing psalms
In the winds of fate?
Hidden in seclusion
Listening in the mineral dark
To the earth's
Global burial rites

Listening to
My mother's green humming
From her grave today,
Her birthday

7

Who are we
   Talking to ourselves
      In the blue clay of consciousness,
         Our soul breaths
            Surrounded by sickness and fear?

We bathe ourselves
   Cut our hair
      Sing to the winds and sky

Joy lives in our spirit house
   That lives inside us.
      Even in the dark times,
         We sip our coffee,
            Joy will never die,
               There will be singing
                  Even in the dark times.

SHELTERING IN PLACE 3

*"If only we were
brave enough to be it"*
-Amanda Gorman

And still more beautiful
  The North Star
    Rising up from the ruins
    Pulses with promise
      From the house of song.

Owls cry out
  From the blue moon of witness,
    Honoring front-line workers'
    Saving grace

Talking to ourselves,
  And singing through masks
    Worn with pride
     Sharing our stay calm lyrics
      Through the forest's thorns.

Who turns herself inside out,
    Living in the shadows of sound,
      As caravans dance through flames
     Falling through the crushed
      Embers of time?

As our human faces
  Deepening with sorrow
   For the world's dead

Rise up
With the wounds of hope
Rise up
Fighting for freedom's song.

NIGHT OF SORROW
NIGHT OF ASH

"Love for love, life for life, death for death"

-Pablo Neruda

Lilacs in the burnt wind
   Spark the soul's migration,
      As we raise our dead communally,
         From the dusk's
            Locked up night.

The changing wind
   Spins her red sash
      Over mass burial trenches
         In the Bronx.
            Darkness sparks the soul's sorrow,
               Sparks the world's ash.

Cé VITA SPERANZA!

HOPE!

Carmela teaches me the Italian word "speranza," Hope!

"Where there's life there's hope,"

"Spes ultima dea"

"Hope is the last goddess"

So the last to die."

Verde Speranza

The ancient's green bird

Flying through Dante's purgatory.

"Non c'essere giú!

Ricordati che finche"

"Don't fall down

Remember there's always hope."[1]

---

1   *FROM L'ITALO AMERICANO FORWARDED TO ME BY POET CARMELA DELIA LANZA.

RETURN

"Return to the root of the root

of your soul"

-Rumi

How will we return
   From this devastation?
What deep-forest wisdom
   Will guide us
      Back from the dead?

How will we sing the memories
   Of those lost
      In the burnt lilac dust
         In the solitude of ash?

Who are we
   If we do not return
   Walking freely
      With compassion and kindness?

If we do not return to the
   Root of our souls,
      Sharing the twilight's
         Sheltered songs?

PANDEMIC

It is winter.

Crows inside the quarantine zone

Oversee evacuees

In the winds of sorrow.

You arrive from Beijing,

Sword Woman,

With your twin children.

We hear your empowered song

As the burnt snow

Blankets the stars.

WHAT KIND OF COUNTRY IS THIS?

Displaced turtles cry

In the shadows of refugees.

Frogs listen to babies

Cry themselves to sleep

As the borders'

Heartless long road

Howls in the deep.

No peace in this dark longing.

The Angel of Death on Furnace Street

Throws us to the winds of life.

Dreams will not protect us

From the poison seeping within.

Blackbirds rattle coffins

In the lies of the day.

Crows bury the dead,

As all is taken away.

LILITH

With flypaper hanging from your wrists
Moor-stalker
In the cemeteries of strangers,
A perpetual fire in your eyes
Knowing the desert's place
Beneath the stars
Running fleet-footed
With poppy seeds and honey cakes.

Way-changer
Running where memory flies like birds
Across the sky
Beneath the trees
Deep into the heart of life.

Your music pulling us backwards into the night
These days of Awe.

Night-walker
With your red sash
In smoke filled rooms,
Blood-born in the gods' excuses
The erotic, born of chaos
Thrown out of the temple for bareness,
The scrolls of prayer
Keening in song.

Letting the music take you
Letting the music play you.

Sounding the shofar from darkness to light,
The intimate sound of death and the river
Life and grief,
Riddling in the year's last sheaf
All that music gives beyond grief.

CHERISH

Lilith's soul of the earth

  Pierced by thunder's salt sea,

    Circles me

      In the wilderness of dreams,

        Running through the winds of forgetting

        With the tablets of fate.

Stepping into the forest's music,

  The twilight of mystery,

    The dark light

      Illumined by pines.

Saying Kaddish,

  The Hebrew prayer for the dead,

    For my father,

      As the moon's gold leaf

        Over our dirt road

          Disappears into the sublime.

WINTER'S LIQUID AMBER

For Carol Heffer

*"Unless we dream into each other,
There can be no garden"*
-Rumi

*"In the sea-depths of music,
We voyage together."*
-Odysseus Elytis

Winter brings the deepest

  Quickest return

    To our subtle, gentlest essences.

    We feel the night

      Fall into our bodies,

      Into our hearts

Listening to the black keys'

  Fire and winds

    Of Art Blakey's *Jazz Messengers,*

    The blood-moon flames

      Of Charlie Parker's sax,

More beautiful,

  Surrounding yourself with yellow roses,

    Remembering Nights in Tunisia,

Womb of the heart

Salt memory of solitude

Thrust open to the sun,

Honey hidden in the winds of faith,

The blue thunder of crows

Rising above,

Your soul light

Licking scarlet from friendship's love.

HARLEQUIN OF MONTMARTRE

For Rosanna Warren
And For Max Jacob (1876-1944)

Harlequin of Montmartre,

Sharing your room with Picasso

On the Boulevard Voltaire,

Raconteur au Bateau Lavoir,

Smoking opium in the ether's fray,

Reeking of tobacco, turpentine, kerosene, henbane,

Reciting *Le Cornet A Dés*

In Yiddish-inflected French,

A renegade Jew,

Reading *The Sefer-Ha-Zohar*,

The Book of Splendor,

Telling fortunes,

With your alchemical world-view,

The Virgin of Guadelupe

Witnessing Picasso's

Les Demoiselles D'Avignon,

A miracle

Before your eyes.

Wearing your yellow star,

   The gestapo dragging you

      To Drancy Transport,

         Dying of pneumonia,

           Dreaming of *ex-voto* light

The *Sefer Yetzira*

   Pulling you into the dark,

The blood-moon of Baal,

   Shining over you,

      Your poetry, your art,

         Lost in the great sorrow.

FALLEN ANGEL

For Rosanna Warren

And for Max Jacob   (1876-1944)

"I wanted a day with cracks,
to let the God-light in"
-Rosanna Warren

"Come ye masters of war,
You who build the big bombs"
-Bob Dylan

Catholic brother of illumination,
  Wandering Jew,
    Kissing men in the lamplight's dark,
    Wearing your penitente
     Bracelet of nails
      Dragged to Drancy's
     Transport Camp,
      Dying of pneumonia
     As the end draws near

Beloved friend,
  Suffering from heartbreak's lust,
   A wingless basilisk,
    Devoted to the imaginative
   Power of Art,

Your Poetry drenched in
  Dirty tears
   From The Rue Ravignan
   And The Bateau Lavoir

Your perfume scented
  With the Power
    To Make Things Happen,
      Evoking the mystical power of words

With Charlie Chaplin
  Reveling in The Avant-Garde's absurd.
    Reading tarot cards,
      The goddess B'al Tamar
        Wrapped around you in scrolls,

Wearing your yellow star
  In the salt-communion of souls
    Remembering the faces
      Of the men you loved,
        Bestowing gifts upon friends
        From your deepest self.

Painting your gouache vision of war,
  Raconteur, troubadour,
    Praying in the ruins of time.

      Picasso couldn't save you,
        Declaring
        "Max is an angel,
          He can fly over the wall
            By himself."

Blessing tobacco, morphine and henbane
  With beggars, and prostitutes,
    When the sky broke open
      As if to speak,
        Falling, falling.

NIGHT LAMENT

For Paul Celan (1920-1970)

> *"Black milk of daybreak we drink it at evening*
> *We drink it at midday and morning*
> *We drink it at night*
> *We drink and we drink."*
> *-Paul Celan from **Death Fugue***

Night of broken glass

Shatters the hidden sacred

Again and again

Memory fragments

Into the mud and clay

Stirred up by incendiary

Smoke of hate

Blue numbers on your arm

Sheltering children

Through blue nights

"Your golden hair Marguerite,

Your ashen hair, Shulamite."

NIGHT 2

For Paul Celan

Your dark soul
   Lost in the wake of dreams,
   Your wounded cry,
      Burnt wind
         Forced labor
            Red star.

Lost in *Death Fugue's* lilac dark,
   Years later
      Drowned in the Seine's sorrow of sun

            Night souls
               Breath to breath
                  Washing the dead
                     At the center of the world.

SHEKINAH IN EXILE

For Elie Wiesel   (1928-2016)

And for Derora Bernstein (1942-1977)

*"Never shall I forget
The small faces of the children
Whose bodies I saw
    transformed into smoke
Under a silent sky."*
    -Elie Wiesel

Wind singing through sacred souls
  Opens the gate,
    "Arbeit Macht Frei"
      Sky tipped to the deep mineral dark
        Piercing the trembling night,
          Shekinah's sacred sparks bury
            Night cries

Witnessing the smoke of extermination's
  Mass-graves
    Through your child-eyes,
      Saying the unspeakable
        As the world remains silent.

Writing in your Yiddish
  Mama loshn
    Mother tongue of Transylvania's
      Small town
        Sighet in Hungary
          Night shrouding Jewish memory.

27

Today, the dead frozen in morgue trailers
  Marked for desecration trenches in the Bronx,
    Bring us back to our grief,
      The blood-star of memory
        Gathering shards,

In the soul psalms of sorrow's smoke,
  Our loved ones left behind,
    Saying the unspeakable
      'Never Again'

Witnessing Confederate flags and
  Camp Auschwitz t-shirts,
    In the dark tremor
      Of insurrection and death.

IN TIBERIUS

For Betsy Levine (1947-2021)

"Speak to me, but speak of tears."

-Odysseus Elytis

A drop of dark wine,

We spill

The salt glaze of tears

Hearts bleed

Into the Book of Splendor,

Dancing Bedouin psalms

Under the olive trees,

Open to death and winds.

Listening to Galeet Dardashti

Singing Mizrahi songs

Dreaming hyacinth winds

Of love and loss,

Dying into the morning

Seeding stars.

BRING US BACK

When I was young,
The light poured from me,
Now the pomegranate dark
Drenches my soul
With *duende's* song.

"Besiege your siege"
-Mahmoud Darwish

BRING US BACK

Bring us back to love's portal
  Back to the green bird of hope
    Speranza
Remembering what we lost
  Exiled in the world's graveyards.

Take us to the river of enchantment
  And renewal
Bring us back to repair
  The broken agates,
    Return to the vision of care.

What will we do with our freedom,
  Wandering with new visions and vows?
    Who are we now?

LILACS IN THE EXILED ASH

"Besiege your siege"

-Mahmoud Darwish

For Mahmoud Darwish (1941-2008)

Lilacs in the exiled ash of forgetting,

Blue moon over

The dispossessed land,

Returning to Ramallah's siege

Of collective memory,

After the bombing of Beirut.

What will you do with your fear?

Your friendship's mystery residing

In the devastation of

Muwashah's * in Bedouin texts?

"When will peace open our citadel doors?

Arms raised to greet the night's

Shadow breath

Of the stranger's *Salaam*

A sorrow song

For the butterfly's sun and wind.

TWILIGHT GHAZAL

For Mahmoud Darwish (1941-2008)

Fleeing Galilee to Lebanon,

  Cairo to Beirut,

    Exiled in Palestine's dispossessed land.

Poet of collective memory's

  Sovereign song,

    Bearing witness to the seige,

      "Besiege your siege,"

        Hoping for Freedom's *Salaam.*

Night stirs,

  As butterfly's sleep

    In the starlit pulse of prayer.

PRAISEPOEM

Praise to you, praise in cloud, in sunray,
in health, in swords,
bleeding front , whose thread of blood
echoes on the deeply wounded stones,
a slipping away of harsh sweetness
bright cradle armed with lightning,
fortress, substance, air of blood,
from which bees are born.[2]
-Pablo Neruda
Residence on Earth

Praise the forest return
  The fire tower
    The willow tent
      The sheltered divine.

Lapis song
  For those
    Shrouded in darkness

Water
  For well-being and care.

Praise the healers,
  The front-line heroes,
    The mercy blues,
      Shattering the vessels of time.

Praise old women chewing garlic.
  On bread lines,
    Mountain deer.

2   NERUDA POEM TRANSLATED BY DONALD WALSH.

36

The rainbow bridge,
  The lemon peel,
    The olive pit,
      The sacred trash,
       ·   The sewing kit.

Praise the Beloved,
  The rubble of distress,
    The soul's last breath.

When will the rain
  Wash clean our wounds
    Revealing
      All we forgot?

Praise the global world kitchens,
  Ghanaian pallbearers,
    New born kittens
      Those who stir the pots.

TALKING DRUM

Birthday Poem For Wahru

At the Indiana Women's Festival
  In Bloomington,
    Women followed you
      Thinking you were Odetta
        Singing
        "Oh Freedom over me."

        "Didn't it rain children,
          Rain all night long,
            Didn't it rain."

We hummed in the dark light of becoming,
  Talking drum heat lightning,
    Talking blues,
      Call and response,
        That sparked our souls.

We laughed
  With red-dirt under our fingernails,
    At the Old Paris Flea-Market,
      As the Winds of Tiger Mountain
        Almost threw us from that cliff
          That Force To Be Reckoned With.

ZOHAR

For Jorge Luis Borges

And for John Coltrane

Return the sparks of life
To the roots of love

Ancient *piyuts*[3]
Blessing the day,
Sing from The Book of Psalms,
The hummingbird chords
Lost to time

As Coltrane's "A Love Supreme"
Undulates in dream winds
Playing sax between worlds
Drinking blue wine.

---

3   ANCIENT JEWISH LITURGICAL PRAYERS.

YEAR OF FORGETTING

Smoke of the wolf

Thunder of the coyote

Fate of the turtle

Heart of the deer

Wish of the woman

Iridescence of the grackle

Glitter of the shadow

Passion of the stone

Weeping of the willow

Roosting of the crow

Cry of the loon.

POET'S SEAT TOWER

Greenfield, Massachusetts

For Dan Carr and Julia Ferrari

We climbed to read our poetry aloud
  To the hemlocks and pines,
    Branching the dark.

Suddenly
  A porcelain toilet
    Was thrown down from the platform,
      Shattering green ash
        On the concrete below.

Blackbirds followed our music
  Moaning absurdity's riffs,
    As night laughed
      In spidery winds

And the trees
  Danced to our
    Leaves of life
      Our rhythms of prayer.

AT MANNY'S BLUES BAR

At Manny's Blues Bar,
  The brothers sing,
    Reminding me,
      "You can't come to the circle
        Three times with the same question,
          Until it screams."

  "Give me one good reason
      That I should make a change.
       I said,
         Give me one good reason,
          That I should make a change."

  "I would not lie to you,
    Or cry to you."

Drinking martinis
  Lost in the dream of forgetting,
    In the underbelly of sound.

THE SHOFAR'S SOULSONG

Your soul rises

Through the ke-yah

Arc of memory

Falling, falling.

The wind turns toward love.

Night and day strikes

A devotional chord

Towards the lilac sky's

Labyrinth of song.

NERUDA'S ISLA NEGRA

> I wheeled with the stars
> My heart broke lose
> with the wind
> Pablo Neruda

Earth music of the soul
  Rivering firefly
    Honey of longing
Cordillera besieged at dawn
  Licking pollen
    In the twilight's fear.

Earth music of dreams
  Sending violet roots
    Through the scarlet mud's
      Deep sea,
        Dreaming the world.

They tore your house down.
  Your Residence on Earth,
    Your Isla Negra
      Your eyelids white from trauma,
        Burning through sulfur
          Of the fascist's blue fires,
            Burning through time.

"...the chairs sing,
the heart cries out without a guitar,
sorrow wanders in a tunnel." [4]

---

4   FROM PABLO NERUDA'S *ISLA NEGRA, A NOTEBOOK.*

Forgetting destiny's dissonant dreams,
Remembering the rain in the pines,
Earth womb of winter bees,
Sparking the raven world's hive.
Heart of mystery
As agates split open.

THE DREAMTIME

Alice Springs, Australia

The ghost-gums dream opals
At the transport station's
Ancestral pool of witness,
Humming songlines
In the shape-shifting
Spirit of rivers,
Owls blessing the land.

In the glow-worm
Waitomo caves of New Zealand,
A young French woman
Who worked in Fiji
Hitchhiked with us,
To a vegetarian restaurant
On the South Island,
Vanishing in the green winds of story.

Tourists climb Ayer's Rock
Invading Uluru's sacred fertility grounds,
Holding onto the chain-link fence
Between worlds,
As aboriginal songs of dreamtime
Pierce tourists
With cries of protest and grief.

WHAT DID YOU LEARN?

What did you learn

  Riding the night's sky roads

    With crows roosting

      Here and there?

As mountain thunder paints the tides,

  Deep violet

    With wolves whelping in storms.

Crawling with poison caterpillars

  And false dragon flowers

    Seeding stars?

What did you learn

  When the night's skyroad

    Crashed into the sea?

IN SANTIAGO DE CHILE

"...having left behind the burning
lights of the forest,
and the tapers of dawn and love."
-Marjorie Agosin

In Santiago de Chile
  The Mothers of the Disappeared
    Listening to the heartbeat music
      Of Devotion's dawn

Fighting for Human Rights'
  Ancestral Song,
    Searching for the lost, the disappeared,
      On the Plaza de Mayo's
        Blue clay,

The talisman of the dead
  On the altar of prayer
    Witnessing
      The mutilated torture
        Of the dead and the living,
          In the gardens of night.

Heart-Womb

"The light inside the new moon,
The terrible grief of being human"
-Rumi

"All acts of kindness are lights
in the war for justice"
-Joy Harjo

SONG

For Bob

Thunder of earth-womb's
  Green pollen

Dark heart of the
  World's compassion
    Reaches for the night.

Why does
  Blue ash
    Cover the roses?

Green pulse
  Of the river's dawn

Gash of iridescence
  In the forest's song.

TRANSCENDENCE

For Hugh and Jeanne Joudry

The corn's blue tassels
  Seed the wind,
    In the blue nights of solitude.

Beautiful, the black butterfly of darkness
  Surrounds us with song,
    Lifting her mask
      To the breath of strangers,
        As we zoom the stars'
          Meditative prayer,
            Viral over graves of mountain hare.

Am I bleeding
  Over blood-root and hepatica,
    Discordant in praise
      For first responders
        Healing the sick
          On the front lines?

Metegwyss, the trickster hare,
  Jumps up high to court his mate,
    Coy,
      Wearing her protective mask,
        His hare lover
          Shelters in place,
            As fireflies loose their spark

As the virus strikes
  Riding through the dark
    Under the eyes
      Of luna moths.

THE TOWER

For Hugh and Jeanne Joudry

Dream-walking in the lilac stream

Of mountain song,

On Manicknung,

Sacred Mountain,

Where the mountains pile up.

Your Tai chi dance

Catches porqupine quills,

As mountain thunder

Surrenders to the calm;

Your alchemy of colts foot, trillium,

Sculpting the green silence.

SOUL-BROTHER

For Gerald McBride

"In the depths of our hearts,
we are together."
-Pablo Neruda

Your soul illumines the night's

Lapis Sky,

A burnt tear that takes

A thousand years to melt into your soul.

Brother of stars and wind,

Brother of fireflies,

Besieged in the twilight.

Soul-brother of We'Wha's wisdom and gifts,

L'hamana of the Sacred Berdache,

Dark night of the Zohar's breath.

Moving through the Sandia

Sands of time.

AWE

For Gerald McBride

For We'Wha (1849-1896)

Grandson of We'Wha,
　Zuni hamana,
　　Embodying the mystery
　　　Of the sacred Berdache,

The mystery of leaves veining crimson,
　The blood jade of earth's beauty,
　　Sparking mountain ash.

　　　Lost in memory's ancestral darkness,
　　　　Lost in memory's ancestral light.

Quetzal of Díos sparking dreams,
　Quetzal of luminous blessings,
　　　Praising luna moths, azul,
　　　　Writing qasidas of light and wind,

Grandson of New Mexico's Governor,
　Armijo (x4)
　　Sparking your
　　　Pueblo green song.

CANTO JONDO

For Gerald McBride

"Because to love and to sing costs dearly"
Becho's Violin, Composed by Alfredo Zitarosa
Translated by Gerald McBride

Wake to the ambers of friendship's deep soul,
  Listening to the beauty of your violin's cry
    Playing *Ave Maria*
      At the Cristo Rae Altar in Santa Fe
      Listening to Becho's violin
        Inspiring us
          In the face of dreams

Pulse-beat
  Of the dissonant sublime
The inner sanctum
  Rising within you
    From your spirit of hope

Living in the spirit of gratitude
  Illumined by Nuestra Señora de la Luz.
Listening to *qasidas*
  Of the angel's deep sky,
    Remembering your Sephardic fires
      Rooted in song,
    Dancing backwards for the
      Days to come.

Salt memory of the *piyyot*
  Spiraling stars,
    Soul-brother of flutes and guitars.

SALT OF THE EARTH

"I wheeled with the stars,
My heart broke loose with the wind."

-Pablo Neruda

Bearing witness to the cordillera wind of stars
   Put out in the burning rain.

Your deep forest
  Temuco roots
    Hidden in liquid fire
     Solitude,
      Pierce
        The sweet gum, liquid embers,
        Blue flames,
         As the full moon
          Shatters its ancient praise.

BUT THE WINDS

For Pablo Neruda

(1904 - 1973)

But the winds' spiral memory
  Sings the deep
    As the summer rains
      Of Valparaiso
        Swing into the future's
      Fire and smoke
      Of forgetting
        Heartbreak's sea-wind blues,
          Shattered by the earthquake's rage.

In the cordillera
  Heart womb of the earth's stone house
    At Isla Negra

As the worm moon celebrates
  The living embers,
    The dark solitude of your soul.

HOUSE OF WINDS

For Remedios Varo

María de los Remedíos Alicia Rodriga Varo (1915 - 1963)

Your alembic astrolabe watched by owls
  Transforms our world,
Your hourglass magic of night's
  Burnt out candles,
Black heart of mystic heartbeat,
  Dreams the wind,
    Conjuring the divine.

Ruby-throated hummingbirds
  Call down the moon,
    Push down into the darkness,
      Pull up into the light,
        Dig down into the mysteries' glass powder,
          Dancing the night-owls song
            As we reach through
            The veils of time.

Women circle your astrolabe of miracles.
  Listening to solar - music soul,
    Your celestial alchemy
      At the Orinoco River,
        Salts the sky.

Spanish sorceress of thunder,
  Nights radiant with life.,
    Draws down light
      From your sanctuary's gash of gold
        In the clouds.

Singing
  The beautiful contradictions,
    Lost in harmonic resonance,
      Of your hidden dark.

Your magnifying glass
  Opening the world to light,
    Moon goddess of beauty's black earth,

Burnt by stars
  Licking scarlet from
    Your towering
      House of winds,

Ascending to "Las Almas de las Montañas",
  "The Spirits of the Mountains,"
    The Virgin of Los Remedíos
      The Virgin of the Remedies,
        Remedios,
          Painting blue doves,
            A new language,
              Ascending to love.

Remedios,
  Your mirror shows
    A fork in the road
      Detour in the labyrinth's
        Celestial earth.

Strike the lightning's wing,
  Sorceress of destiny,
    As sisters eat snails for lunch,

An alchemy of birds
    In your pointed hat,
        Sprinkle marble dust...
            The red thread of fate
            In your palm,

A good omen,
    As fireflies spark the night
        With longing.

SUNLIGHT AND STARS

For Leonora Carrington (1917 - 2011)

Horses haunt your spirit,
   Your convulsive beauty,
      In the painted flames of life's
         Rocking horse apparition,
            Down Below and Above.

Your tapered ankles
   Invoking your horse-warrior self,
      Dreams sunlight and stars,
         Your wild mane
            In your mysterious hyena laugh,
               Your House of Fear.

Risk-taking Goddess of the new moon's
   Tower of mirror-writing
      Inside and out,
         Far away and near.,
            On the bear corridor,
               In the firelight of song.

Winds sing through
   Sacred trash,
      As crows roost,
         Opening the door,
            To the deep mineral dark.

WILD SISTER

For Frida Kahlo (1907-1954)

*First published in **Rattle**, Cardinal Press, 1982.*

You growl in the yucca
You hide out in the tundra
You gallop through the pampas
You carry death winds
             Wide open in the darkness
You wear a necklace of flowers
Your mesa voice hollerin' in snakeroot hoots and drums.

You are the wolf-woman clutching roses,
Your eyes crafty with witchcraft gnaw on tombstones
You sulk in barrios
Your far away grin stabs sunsets
In willow of underground rivers
You ride out from the sunbaked womb
Blind in the dry heat of monkeys
You suckle the belly of beats

You ride out on the mountains
          Ghosting the foothills
           The half moon bent on destruction:
Carry small birds in your rattle-gourd ribcage
Erratic as jackals
Dance salsa in shadows

You are the dog-rose rooting herself in dust
Inside the shadows chewing cactus, chewing sticks
Ecstasy, the fierce light clutching santos   anger pulled off
Childless yourself, the mother of us all

65

Painting a tyranny of sunsets
Your heart a blood-cocoon pierced with a twig
I stroke your starry palette,
Paint *retablos* steel blue fluting your bones

You fling yourself on your bed of bees
Scorched in the open   your womanhood
You growl at the yucca
You hide out in the tundra
You gallop through the pampas
You carry death winds
                    Wide open in the darkness
Sing *corridos* for La Raza
Fleshing a portrait   sister
Where the blood wind drips your name.

THE RUINS OF THE HEART

For Frida Kahlo

Ex-voto
    Blood-star of the divine,
      Retablo of memory,
        Sparking
          Twilight psalms,

Blood ribbons around a bomb,
    Healing your love for Diego,
      By finding the truths in yourself.

      Tree of Life,
        Chthonic in the underworld,
         Weeps from the deep,
        Your heart of fire
         Wounded by grief,

      Your *calavera* canopy
      Over your bed
        Do you hear?

WHO ARE WE NOW?

For Bob

Womb—heart

Earth—Womb

Heart of night

Heat of fireflies,

Harmony of Winds

Pine-pitch of grackle iridescence

Sparking deer,

Tree of life,

Tree of Love.

SHEKINAH'S BREATH

Who, coming out of stories,
  Hears the night
    Pulsing in the mother tongue's
     Divine absence which is presence?

Listening to zimzum,
  The letting free,
    Revealing what is hidden,
     Under the pink moon.

The indwelling of spirit
  Shatters the winds of praise,
    Returning the holy sparks,
     The particles of soul,
      To their resting place,
       Beneath desert stars.

At Tiberius and The Red Sea,
  Listening to bees singing
    From their honeycomb hive,
    Fallen angels
     Cry out
      Like crows
       In their beautiful forgetting.

About the Author

Fallen Angels is Terry Hauptman's seventh volume of poetry, adding to her six previous full length poetry collections: *Masquerading In Clover: Fantasy of the Leafy Fool,* with hand-painted plates (Boston: Four Zoas, 1980), *Rattle* (Tulsa: Cardinal Press, 1982), *On Hearing Thunder* (St Cloud, Minnesota: North Star Press, 2004), *The Indwelling of Dissonance*, (St Cloud, Minnesota: North Star Press, 2016), *The Tremulous Seasons*, (St Cloud, Minnesota: North Star Press, 2019), and her most recent, *Rubies in the Mud* (St Cloud, Minnesota: North Star Press, 2020). She holds a Master's Degree in Poetry from The University of New Mexico, Albuquerque—where she studied with poet laureate, Joy Harjo—and a Ph.D in Interdisciplinary Arts from Ohio University. She reads her poetry rhapsodically and exhibits her luminous 5'x40' Songline Scrolls nationally. She has taught World Art, Poetry, and Ethnopoetics at several universities and workshops, most recently at Green Mountain College. She lives in Vermont with Robert and Kira.